祝你有

Have a Bad Day!

糟糕的一天

Pieni pahan mielen kirja

專為每個想抱怨的人量身打造

作者／洛塔·索妮南（Lotta Sonninen）
繪圖／琵雅·阿賀（Piia Aho）
譯者／吳妍儀

DEAR READER,

I hope you are in a really bad mood today. Do you know why? Because I believe bad moods are good for you. We are often told to focus on the positive things in life and try to leave behind all the negative. But isn't that a waste of energy? We put so much power in our negative feelings. Anger, envy, jealousy, bitterness... they are all packed full of force that can be released and enjoyed. This is what this book is for.

I hope you'll enjoy listing the things and people you hate the most and bravely looking back into your own regrets. It might be liberating, it might be empowering, it might be just a pastime, a bit like a crossword puzzle – but it might also be very funny. Personally, I've noticed that focusing on the negative often makes me laugh – sometimes at myself.

I was surprised at first when it turned out that this book raised interest in many other countries besides my native Finland. Now I understand that if anything is universal, it has to be bad mood. I'm afraid I don't know very much about Taiwan, but I'm pretty sure there is a lot of bad mood to be enjoyed in your country too. Thank you for choosing The Little Book of Bad Moods. I wish you a very good bad mood!

Yours
Lotta Sonninen

親愛的讀者：

　　我希望你今天心情真的很糟。你知道為什麼嗎？因為我相信壞心情對你來說是好的。通常別人會告訴我們，要聚焦於生活中的正面事物之上，還要設法把所有負面事物拋諸腦後。不過那樣不是很浪費精力嗎？我們在自己的負面感受中置入了莫大的力量啊。憤怒、羨慕、嫉妒、怨恨……它們全都滿載著可以被釋放、被享受的飽滿力道。本書就是為此而生。

　　我希望你會樂於列出你最討厭的人事物，並且勇敢地回顧你自己悔恨的事。這樣可能很有解放效果、可能讓人充滿力量、可能只是個消遣，有點像是填字遊戲——但這樣也可能非常有趣。就我個人而言，我已經注意到聚焦於負面事物通常會讓我笑出來——有時候是笑我自己。

　　起初我很驚訝，因為在我的家鄉芬蘭以外的許多其他國家都對這本書很有興趣。現在我理解到如果有任何事情算是世界通行的，肯定就是壞心情了。恐怕我對臺灣所知不多，但我相當確定，在你的國家裡也有很多可以享用的壞心情。

　　感謝你選擇《祝你有糟糕的一天》。祝你有非常好的壞心情！

你的

洛塔・索妮南

目錄
Contents

怪別人

BLAME OTHERS

列出你的伴侶哪裡**不對**。
List what's wrong with your partner.

✗
- -

✗
- -

✗
- -

✗
- -

✗
- -

列出你的小孩哪裡**不對**。
List what's wrong with your kids.

✗
- -

✗
- -

✗
- -

✗
- -

✗
- -

✗
- -

列出你的老闆哪裡**不對**。
List what's wrong with your boss.

✗ --

✗ --

✗ --

✗ --

✗ --

列出你的父母哪裡**不對**。
List what's wrong with your parents.

✗ --

✗ --

✗ --

✗ --

✗ --

✗ --

你的朋友們哪些地方讓你惱火？
What annoys you about your friends?

姓名(NAME)	錯處(FAULTS)

哪個前老闆／同事／員工到現在還讓你火大？為什麼？
What former boss/colleague/employee still makes you angry and why?

你現在還恨你的哪個前任？為什麼？
Which of your exes do you still hate and why?

你如何**在超市結帳隊伍**裡發現一個白痴？
How do you spot an idiot in the supermarket queue?

你如何發現有個白痴**沿路走來**？
How do you spot an idiot walking along the pavement?

你如何**在一間餐廳**裡發現一個白痴？
How do you spot an idiot in a restaurant?

你如何**在約會**時發現一個白痴？
How do you spot an idiot on a date?

你如何**在車流**中發現一個白痴？
How do you spot an idiot in traffic?

- -

- -

- -

你如何**在出國旅行**時發現一個白痴？
How do you spot an idiot abroad?

- -

- -

- -

你如何**在社群網站**上發現一個白痴？
How do you spot an idiot on social media?

- -

- -

- -

你如何**在工作**上發現一個白痴？
How do you spot an idiot at work?

- -

- -

- -

我在**工作**上遇到的白痴們：
Idiots I've met at work:

我在**街頭**遇到的白痴們：
Idiots I've met in the street:

我在**約會**時遇到的白痴們：
Idiots I've met on dates:

我在**酒吧**裡遇到的白痴們：
Idiots I've met at bars:

- -

- -

- -

- -

我在**學校**遇到的白痴們：
Idiots I've met at school:

- -

- -

- -

- -

我在**線上碰到**的白痴們：
Idiot's I've met online:

- -

- -

- -

- -

列出某些熟人或名人，他們……
List acquaintances or celebrities who ...

……太輕鬆就擁有一切
...have had it way too easy

✗

✗

✗

✗

……把自己想得太了不起
...think too much of themselves

✗

✗

✗

✗

……根本不知道什麼對自己最好
...have no idea what's best for them

✗

✗

✗

✗

……就該回學校去 多唸點書
...should just go back to school

✕

✕

✕

✕

……開口前應該多想一想
...should think more before opening their mouth

✕

✕

✕

✕

徹底令人不爽到極點的那種人是……
The absolutely most annoying type of person is

你的老闆最惱人的習慣
Your boss's most irritating habit

你的伴侶最惱人的習慣
Your partner's most irritating habit

你的老師最惱人的習慣
Your teacher's most irritating habit

你的小孩最惱人的習慣
Your child's most irritating habit

你的阿嬤最惱人的習慣
Your grandmother's most irritating habit

你的鄰居最惱人的習慣
Your neighbor's most irritating habit

電視上最惱人的事情
The most irritating thing about TV

政治上最惱人的事情
The most irritating thing about politics

點名開罵

NAME NAMES

你的人生哪裡出了錯？

What's wrong with your life?

出錯的地方 **(WHAT'S WRONG)**

這是誰的錯? (WHOSE FAULT IS IT?)

列出那些**才華比不上你**，卻還是比你成功的人。
Make a list of people who are less talented than you but still more successful.

✗ _____

✗ _____

✗ _____

✗ _____

✗ _____

✗ _____

✗ _____

✗ _____

✗ _____

✗ _____

✗ _____

✗ _____

我嫉妒······
I'm jealous of ...

姓名(**N A M E**)　　　　　理由(**R E A S O N**)

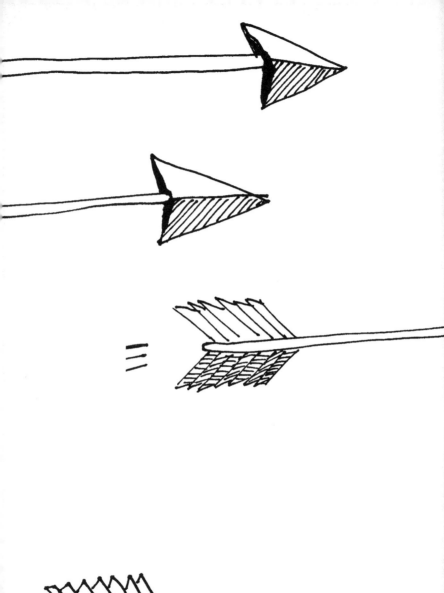

一吐為快

SPEAK YOUR MIND

多數人都不懂這些簡單到極點的事情：

Most people don't understand these extremely simple things:

舉出四個你很樂意訓斥一番的人

Name four people you'd like to **TELL OFF**.

用這些對話框來
好好教訓他們。
USE THE SPEECH BUBBLES
TO GIVE THEM A PIECE
OF YOUR MIND.

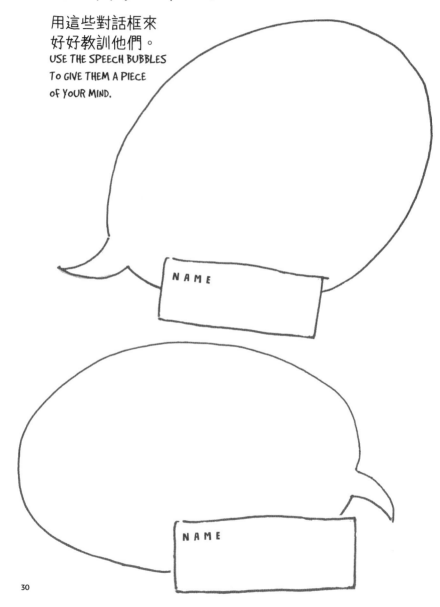

NAME

NAME

寫張**惡毒的紙條**給你煩人的鄰居。
Write your irritating neighbor A NASTY NOTE.

寫個訊息給你**仍然痛恨**的前任老師／同學／同事。
Write a message to the former teacher/classmate/colleague you still hate.

寫個訊息給**曾經侮辱過**你的人。

Write a message to a person who once insulted you.

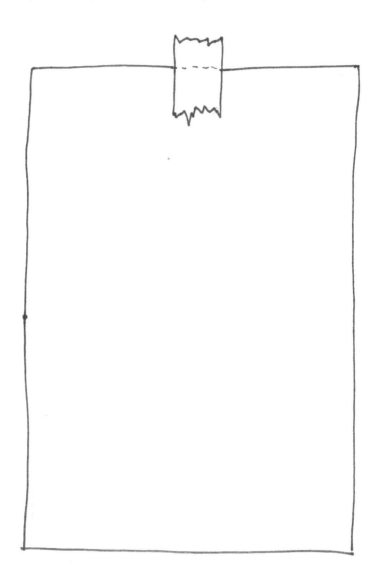

寫個訊息給你仍舊覺得是個**渾蛋的前任**。
Write a message to the ex you still think is a jerk.

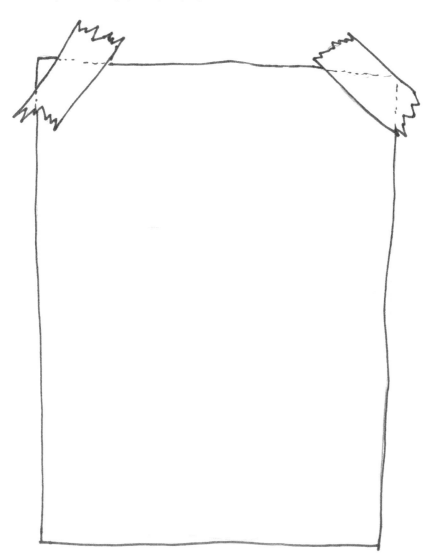

傳送你的怨念

CHANNEL YOUR BITTERNESS

想出三種方式惹惱**你的伴侶**
Think of three ways to irritate your partner

-

-

-

想出三種方式惹惱**你的父母**
Think of three ways to irritate your parents

-

-

-

想出三種方式惹惱**你的同事**
Think of three ways to irritate your colleagues

-

-

-

想出三種方式惹惱**你的老闆**
Think of three ways to irritate your boss

-

-

-

想出三種方式惹惱**你的旅伴**
Think of three ways to irritate your fellow travelers

-

-

-

想出三種在**線上**惹毛別人的方式
Think of three ways to be irritating online

-

-

-

填滿空白處 (FILL IN THE BLANKS)

如果 ＿＿＿＿＿＿ 沒有這麼 ＿＿＿＿＿＿，我的人生
就會輕鬆許多。

如果 ＿＿＿＿＿ 沒有總是 ＿＿＿＿＿，這個世界
會變得更美好。

＿＿＿＿＿＿ 甚至不能 ＿＿＿＿＿，然而他／她總
是 ＿＿＿＿＿。

每次 ＿＿＿＿＿ 開始講到他的／她的 ＿＿＿＿＿
的時候，我都無聊到失智了。

下次 ＿＿＿＿＿ 又開始要 ＿＿＿＿＿ 的時候，我
就要抓狂了。

我根本不知道我為什麼竟然會跟 ＿＿＿＿＿ 一起
＿＿＿＿＿。

我真不知道為什麼 ＿＿＿＿＿ 竟然會被發明出來。

我真不懂為什麼男人總是非得要 ＿＿＿＿＿。

我真不懂為什麼女人總是非得要＿＿＿＿＿＿＿。

我真不懂為什麼小孩總是非得要＿＿＿＿＿＿＿。

我真不懂為什麼＿＿＿＿＿＿總是非得要＿＿＿＿＿＿＿
＿＿＿＿＿＿＿。

老天爺啊都二十一世紀了，為什麼＿＿＿＿＿＿仍
然是＿＿＿＿＿＿＿。

如果我早知道＿＿＿＿＿＿，我絕對不會＿＿＿＿＿
＿＿＿＿＿＿＿。

所有＿＿＿＿＿＿都是白痴，因為他們
＿＿＿＿＿＿＿。

如果可以由我決定，我會禁止＿＿＿＿＿＿去做
＿＿＿＿＿＿＿。

如果可以由我決定，地球上的＿＿＿＿＿＿都會被
消滅。

41

天天都是糟糕日

ANY DAY IS A BAD DAY

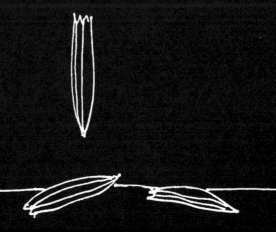

列出這星期有哪裡不對。

List what was wrong with this week.

	把我惹惱的是…… **I WAS ANNOYED BY**	毀了今天的是…… **RUINED THE DAY**
星期一 **MONDAY**		
星期二 **TUESDAY**		
星期三 **WEDNESDAY**		

星期四
THURSDAY

星期五
FRIDAY

星期六
SATURDAY

星期日
SUNDAY

我的惡夢之旅

THE TRIP OF MY NIGHTMARES

地點 (Location)：

人物 (People)：

活動 (Activities)：

發生的事 (What happened)：

地獄聖誕節／跨年／情人節／春節

THE CHRISTMAS/NEW YEAR/VALENTINE DAY/CHINESE NEW YEAR FROM HELL

地點 (Location)：

人物 (People)：

活動 (Activities)：

發生的事 (What happened)：

寫個「不感恩」日記！
KEEP AN INGRATITUDE JOURNAL!

列出這一週**惹毛你**的每件事。
List everything that bothered you this week.

星期一惹毛我的是……
on Monday I was annoyed by ...

星期二惹毛我的是……
on Tuesday I was annoyed by ...

星期三惹毛我的是……
on Wednesday I was annoyed by ...

星期四惹毛我的是……
on Thursday I was annoyed by ...

星期五惹毛我的是……
on Friday I was annoyed by ...

星期六惹毛我的是……
on Saturday I was annoyed by ...

星期日惹毛我的是……
on Sunday I was annoyed by ...

去他X的社群網站

LIFE SUCKS ON SOCIAL MEDIA

令人火大的最新動態

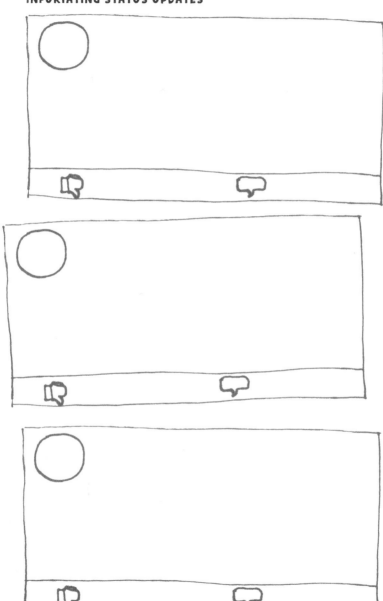

最蠢的留言 (Stupidest comments)

Insta 嘔爛 (Instacrap)

最蠢的推文
Most birdbrained tweets

臉最欠打的表情符號
Emojis that need to be punched in the face

史上最慘的電腦問題
Worst computer trouble

最無腦的網路新聞
Most brainless internet news

畫一些表達**憤怒**或**失望**的新表情符號

Draw new emojis to express rage or frustration

用這個空間寫下你想寄卻永遠不敢寄出的電子郵件。
Use this space to write emails you wish you could send but won't ever dare.

X

收件者TO:

副本CC:

主旨SUBJECT:

収件者 TO:

副本 CC:

主旨 SUBJECT:

✕　　　　　　　　　　　➤

収件者TO:

副本CC:

主旨SUBJECT:

📎 🗓️

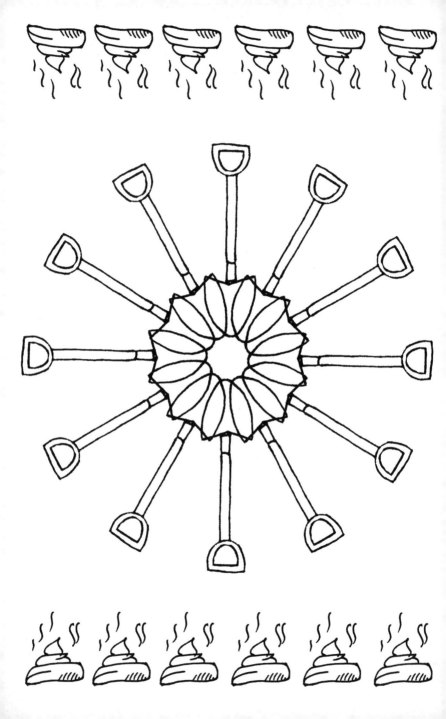

決不遺忘，
死不原諒！

NO FORGETTING, NO FORGIVING

我最後悔的是⋯⋯
I MOST REGRET...

我絕對不原諒……

I'LL NEVER FORGIVE...

我仍舊很不爽的是……

I'M STILL BITTER ABOUT...

列出你到事情結束以後，才想到「早知道應該這樣說」的狀況

List situations where you didn't think of a good comeback until it was over.

時間、地點與人物 **TIME, PLACE AND PEOPLE**	早知道應該這樣說 **PERFECT COMEBACK**

時間、地點與人物
TIME, PLACE AND PEOPLE

早知道應該這樣説
PERFECT COMEBACK

最糟的**旅行災難**
Worst travel disaster

--- ---

--- ---

--- ---

最糟的**感情災難**
Worst relationship disaster

--- ---

--- ---

--- ---

最糟的**服裝災難**
Worst wardrobe disaster

--- ---

--- ---

--- ---

最糟的**烹飪災難**
Worst cooking disaster

--- ---

--- ---

--- ---

最糟的**廁所災難**
Worst toilet disaster

_____

_____

_____

最糟的**DIY災難**
Worst DIY disaster

_____

_____

_____

最糟的**電子郵件災難**
Worst email disaster

_____

_____

_____

最糟的**童年災難**
Worst childhood disaster

_____

_____

_____

最糟的**上台回憶**
Worst memory of being on stage

- -

- -

- -

最糟的**學校回憶**
Worst memory of school

- -

- -

- -

最糟的**更衣室回憶**
Worst changing room memory

- -

- -

- -

最糟的**看病回憶**
Worst memory of the doctor

- -

- -

- -

最糟的**看牙醫回憶**
Worst memory of the dentist

最糟的**約會回憶**
Worst memory from a date

最糟的**打工回憶**
Worst memory of a part-time job

跟父母談話的最糟回憶
Worst memory of talking to your parents

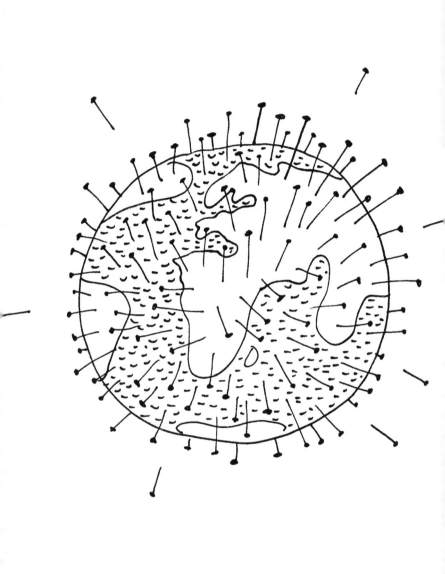

找出世界的
黑暗面

FIND THE BAD IN THE WORLD

是什麼**毀了工作**？
What ruins work?

是什麼**毀了你的早餐**？
What ruins your breakfast?

是什麼**毀了一趟車程**？
What ruins a road trip?

是什麼**毀了一趟巴士旅行**？
What ruins a bus ride?

是什麼**毀了一趟飛機航程**？
What ruins a flight?

是什麼**毀了一頓餐廳大餐**？
What ruins a meal in a restaurant?

是什麼**毀了一場電影**？
What ruins a movie?

是什麼**毀了一杯茶**？
What ruins a cup of tea?

是什麼**毀了一個新髮型**？
What ruins a new haircut?

是什麼**毀了一個平日的夜晚**？
What ruins a weeknight?

是什麼**毀了一齣電視節目**？
What ruins a tv show?

是什麼**毀了一本書**？
What ruins a book?

是什麼**毀了一個假日的夜晚**？
What ruins a holiday night?

是什麼**毀了一趟海灘之旅**？
What ruins a beach trip?

是什麼**毀了一趟血拼之行**？
What ruins a spending spree?

是什麼**毀了一次健身訓練**？
What ruins a workout?

城市裡最氣人的是什麼？
What's most irritating in the city?

鄉下最氣人的是什麼？
What's most irritating in the countryside?

政府最氣人的是什麼？
What's most irritating about the government?

你在報上讀到最氣人的是什麼？
What's the most irritating thing you read in the papers?

廣播裡最氣人的是什麼？
What's most irritating about the radio?

社會上最氣人的是什麼？
What's most irritating about society?

最氣人的**法律**是什麼？
What's the most irritating law?

小孩子哪裡最讓你心煩？
What annoys you about kids?

- -

- -

- -

青少年哪裡最讓你心煩？
What annoys you about teenagers?

- -

- -

- -

大人哪裡最讓你心煩？
What annoys you about adults?

- -

- -

- -

老人哪裡最讓你心煩？
What annoys you about the elderly?

- -

- -

- -

動物哪裡最讓你心煩？
What annoys you about animals?

你自己哪裡最讓你心煩？
What annoys you about you?

這本書哪裡最讓你心煩？
What annoys you about this book?

我最不喜歡的**天氣**是……
My least favorite weather is ...

我最不喜歡的**食物**是……
My least favorite food is ...

我最不喜歡的**飲料**是……
My least favorite drink is ...

最沒意義的**觀光勝地**是……
The most pointless tourist attraction is ...

最蠢的**娛樂形式**是……
The stupidest form of entertainment is ...

最爛的**音樂**是……
The worst music is ...

最爛的**家務**是……
The worst domestic chore is ...

最蠢的**運動種類**是……
The stupidest kind of exercise is ...

最荒謬的**服裝**是……
The most ridiculous piece of clothing is ...

最侮辱人的**讚美**是……
The most offensive compliment is ...

 畫出某個愚蠢沒意義的玩意

DRAW SOMETHING STUPID AND POINTLESS

最廢的**發明**是……
The most pointless invention is ...

最廢的**嗜好**是……
The most pointless hobby is ...

最廢的**工作**是……
The most pointless job is ...

最廢的**動物**是……
The most pointless animal is ...

最廢的**座右銘**是……
The most pointless motto is ...

最廢的**對話主題**是……
The most pointless conversation topic is ...

最**浪費錢**的事情是……
The biggest waste of money is ...

這樣做很**丟臉**……
It's embarrassing to …

這樣做很**荒謬**……
It's ridiculous to …

這樣做很**幼稚**……
It's childish to …

這樣做很**粗魯**……
It's rude to …

這樣做真的**很挫**……
It's really awkward to …

這樣做**不可原諒**……
It's unforgivable to …

這種做法被**捧得太高**了……
It's overrated to …

列出所有你以前忍受過、現在正在忍受、或者害怕將來可能要忍受的**長痛**、**短痛**、**身痛**、**心痛**。

List all the aches and pains you have ever suffered from, suffer from now, or fear you may suffer from in the future.

讓你的用詞
更惡毒

BADDEN YOUR VOCABULARY

煩死了、討人厭、超挫折……
IRRITATING , ANNOYING, FRUSTRATING, ...

繼續寫下去！
continue the list!

北七、腦殘、蠢貨……

IDIOT, BUFFOON, MORON ...

繼續寫下去！
continue the list!

用不同的字體寫下粗話跟辱罵用詞

WRITE SWEAR WORDS AND INSULTS IN DIFFERENT
HANDWRITING

你怎麼不去……

吃……

寫下你知道的所有外文粗話。

Write all the swearwords you know in a foreign language.

寫下你知道的所有中文粗話。

Write all the swearwords you know in Chinese.

你**最痛恨**哪句流行語？
What buzzwords do you most hate?

哪種老套**最老套**？
Which clichés are most clichéd?

哪些字眼讓你覺得**最反感**？
What words do you find most revolting?

哪些「智慧小語」**最北七**？
What' words of wisdom' are most inane?

無腦混混才用的字眼
Words only ever used by ignorant hooligans

勢利小人才用的字眼
Words only ever used by pretentious snobs

小屁孩才用的字眼
Words only ever used by teenagers

老不死才用的字眼
Words only ever used by old fossils

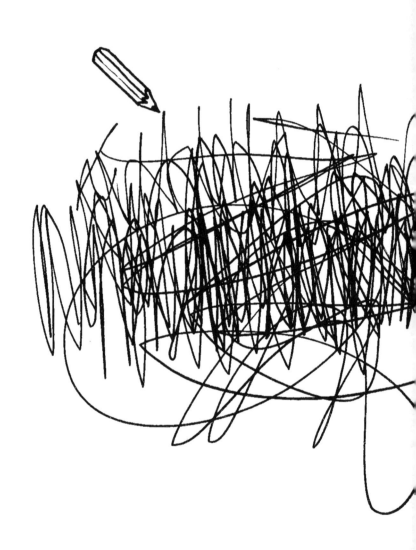

劃清界線

DRAW THE LINE

替這個巫毒娃娃畫張臉，或者其他突出的特徵。

Give this voodoo doll a face or other distinguishing features.

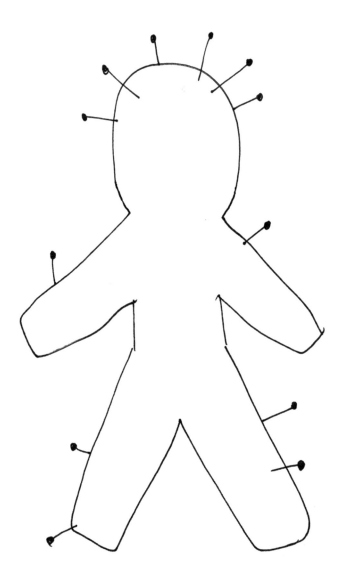

畫一隻真正醜翻的動物。

Draw a really ugly animal.

畫出輪廓並著色
DRAW AND COLOR

 一套粗俗的服裝

a gross outfit

畫出輪廓並著色
DRAW AND COLOR

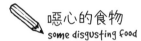

噁心的食物
some disgusting food

畫出一個交通號誌，禁止你痛恨的某種東西。

DRAW A TRAFFIC SIGN TO FORBID SOMETHING YOU HATE.

設計某款醜爆的壁紙。

DESIGN SOME UGLY WALLPAPER.

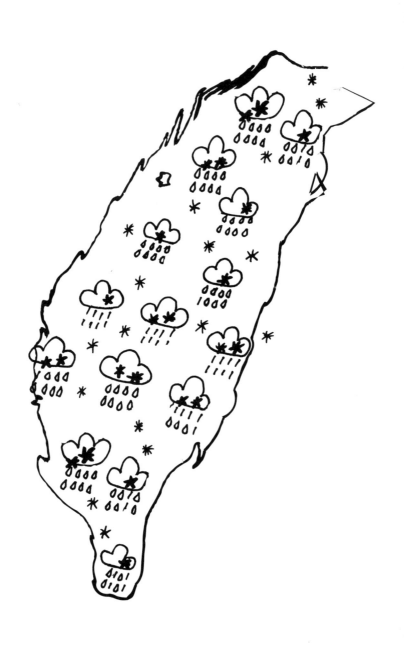

恨到底

HATE IT UP

我痛恨 I HATE...

☐ 聖誕節 (Christmas)
☐ 新年 (New Year)
☐ 我的生日 (My birthday)
☐ 國定假日 (Bank holidays)
☐ _____
因為 _____
_____

☐ 公共運輸 (Public transport)
☐ 汽車 (Cars)
☐ 行人 (Pedestrians)
☐ 單車騎士 (Cyclists)
☐ _____
因為 _____
_____

☐ 痘痘 (Pimples)
☐ 黑眼圈 (Dark circles)
☐ 眼袋 (Eye bags)
☐ 頭皮屑 (Dandruff)
☐ _____
因為 _____
_____

☐ 春天 (Spring)
☐ 夏天 (Summer)
☐ 秋天 (Autumn)
☐ 冬天 (Winter)
☐ _____
因為 _____
_____

☐ 狗 (Dogs)
☐ 貓 (Cats)
☐ 天竺鼠 (Guinea pigs)
☐ 寵物主人 (Pet owners)
☐ _____
因為 _____
_____

☐ 籃球 (Basketball)
☐ 登山 (Mountain climbing)
☐ 棒球 (Baseball)
☐ 馬拉松 (Marathon)
☐ _____
因為 _____
_____

☐ 饒舌樂 (Rap)
☐ 搖滾樂 (Rock music)
☐ 流行樂 (Pop songs)
☐ 古典樂 (Classical music)
☐ _____
因為 _____
_____

☐ 香菜 (coriander)
☐ 苦瓜 (Bitter gourd)
☐ 茄子 (Eggplant)
☐ 青椒 (Green pepper)
☐ _____
因為 _____

☐ 賀年卡 (Round robin letters)
☐ 布告欄 (Notice boards)
☐ 社區會議 (community meetings)
☐ 人 (People)
☐ _____
因為 _____

☐ 英文 (English)
☐ 體育 (P.E.)
☐ 數學 (Math)
☐ 化學 (chemistry)
☐ _____
因為 _____

我痛恨 I HATE ...
☐ _____
☐ _____
☐ _____
☐ _____
☐ _____
因為 _____

☐ 蕾絲洋裝 (Lace dress)
☐ 西裝領帶 (Suits and ties)
☐ 緊身褲 (tights)
☐ 連身衣 (onesies)
☐ _____
因為 _____

☐ 掃地 (Sweeping the floor)
☐ 洗碗 (Washing up)
☐ 熨衣服 (Ironing)
☐ 拖地 (Mopping the floor)
☐ _____
因為 _____

人生顧問0361

祝你有糟糕的一天—— 專為每個想抱怨的人量身打造

作　者－洛塔‧索妮南
繪　圖－琵雅‧阿賀
譯　者－吳妍儀
主　編－林菁菁、林潔欣
編　輯－黃凱怡
企劃主任－葉蘭芳
美術設計－李宜芝

發行人－趙政岷
出版者－時報文化出版企業股份有限公司
　　　　10803台北市和平西路三段240號3樓
　　　　發行專線－(02)2306-6842
　　　　讀者服務專線－0800-231-705‧(02)2304-7103
　　　　讀者服務傳真－(02)2304-6858
　　　　郵撥－19344724 時報文化出版公司
　　　　信箱－台北郵政79-99信箱
時報悅讀網－http://www.readingtimes.com.tw
法律顧問－理律法律事務所 陳長文律師、李念祖律師
印　刷－盈昌印刷有限公司
初版一刷－2019年04月19日
定　價－新台幣320元

時報文化出版公司成立於一九七五年，
並於一九九九年股票上櫃公開發行，於二〇〇八年脫離中時集團非屬旺中，
以「尊重智慧與創意的文化事業」為信念。

祝你有糟糕的一天：專為每個想抱怨的人量身打造/洛塔‧索妮南著；
琵雅‧阿賀繪；吳妍儀譯. -- 初版. -- 臺北市：時報文化, 2019.04
　　面； 公分
譯自：Pieni pahan mielen kirja
ISBN 978-957-13-7761-2(精裝)

1.自我實現 2.生活指導

177.2　　　　　　　　　　　　　　　　　　　　108004385

Pieni pahan mielen kirja by Lotta Sonninen Copyright text © Lotta Sonninen, 2018
Copyright work © Otava Publishers, 2018 Original edition published by Otava, 2018
Cover, graphic design and illustrations by Otava Publishing Company Ltd. / Piia Aho
Complex Chinese edition published by agreement with Lotta Sonninen and Elina Ahlback Literary Agency,
Helsinki, Finland
Complex Chinese edition copyright © 2019 by China Times Publishing Company
All rights reserved.

ISBN：978-957-13-7761-2
Printed in Taiwan